A KLONDIKE SCRAPBOOK

Clarence Kinsey *(second from left)* and Clarke's wife, Mary, *(fourth from left)* stop with their friends on the boardwalk along the main street of Grand Forks.

A KLONDIKE SCRAPBOOK

Ordinary People, Extraordinary Times

Norman Bolotin

Chronicle Books • San Francisco

Library of Congress cataloging in publication data available.

First printing 1987 10 9 8 7 6 5 4 3 2 1   Printed in Singapore by Tien Wah Press

Design and production by Laing Communications Inc., Bellevue, Washington

Chief copy editor/editorial research -- Delia Ray Howard
Additional copyediting -- Christine A. Laing
Design and layout -- Sandra J. Harner

All Kinsey & Kinsey photographs are from the collection of Ronald C. Kinsey, Jr., unless otherwise noted.

Distributed in Canada by Raincoast Books
112 East Third Avenue
Vancouver, British Columbia V5T 1C8

Chronicle Books
One Hallidie Plaza
San Francisco, California 94102

For Jacob and Zachary

May they find happiness, adventure and
whatever Eldorado they seek.

Contents

Introduction

As a magazine editor in the early 1970s writing about a variety of subjects, including business in Alaska, I became fascinated with Alaska and Klondike history. Jack Wills, then employed in *The Seattle Times* photography department, knew of my interest and introduced me to Ronald C. Kinsey, Jr., grandson of Clarke Kinsey. Clarke, like his brother Darius, left an incredible legacy of logging photography spanning nearly half of the twentieth century. He also left a limited, but uniquely descriptive photographic

Edmund and Louisa Kinsey with their children, circa 1885; Klondike photographer Clarke is seated at the far left and Clarence stands at the far right.

history of the Klondike, which went undiscovered for many years.

Long after the gold rush and long after the death of the Kinsey brothers in the 1950s, Jack and Ron, his neighbor, began sorting through dusty crates of glass plate negatives that survived the Klondike and various family moves. That Kinsey photographic legacy was the impetus for my 1980 book *Klondike Lost: A Decade of Photographs by Kinsey and Kinsey* and plays an integral part in this book as well.

Clarke and the older Darius became business partners in the latter years of the nineteenth century and traveled Western Washington and the Greater Seattle area, specializing in portrait and business photography and serving as official photographers for The Snoqualmie, Lakeshore & Eastern Railroad.

Darius struck out on his own and quickly established himself as one of the premier industrial photographers on the West Coast. A second Kinsey and Kinsey partnership was soon formed, as Clarke and another brother, Clarence, decided to join the Klondike gold rush.

The Kinsey studio in Grand Forks, among the many log and clapboard buildings in the Klondike, foreshadows architectural styles of the future. The huge window was rare, both for its design, which accommodated the photographers' need for light in their studio, and the extravagance of such a possession. Glass was almost unheard of in the Klondike until about 1899 when the mining towns began to sport the luxuries brought north by enterprising businessmen. Photographers Clarke *(second from bottom)* and Clarence *(immediately above him)* pose on the stairs of their studio.

While the Kinseys were excellent industrial and logging photographers, they were not the only men of their trade to profit from their journey to the Klondike. During the gold rush boom of 1898, dozens of enterprising photographers headed for Dawson City and surrounding areas, remaining in the Yukon Territory throughout the gold era. Most photographers concentrated on the struggle of would-be

miners over the Chilkoot and White passes, while the Kinseys focused on everyday life in Dawson and the nearby town of Grand Forks-- the briefly glorious bedroom community fourteen miles from Dawson.

The Kinseys became citizens of the Klondike. They raised their families, worked their mines and took part in the small-town life at "the Forks," where Ethel Russell Moyer, Jim Kingsley and Olive Kinsey Powers once lived as children.

Many years later, after enough time and distance grew between those children and the Klondike to make them cherish their experiences there, I was fortunate enough to hear their stories. Their memories, along with other personal accounts and excerpts from that time, add color to the stage which was set in *Klondike Lost*. While that first volume is a history of the time and place those rich photographic images portray, *A Klondike Scrapbook* is meant to bring life to the faces found in the photographs.

Every book, regardless of its genre, is far more than a manuscript. It is a puzzle consisting of many bits and pieces, *hopefully* falling together to tell a poignant story worthy of the people who actually experienced it. For all those interested in history, the Klondike and the ordinary people who lived there, I hope this scrapbook--this photographic essay--provides the vehicle for several brief and enjoyable excursions back in time.

--Norman Bolotin

SLUICEING ON ADAMS HILL

A Fever for Eldorado

The gold mines of the Klondike should have been singled out for nineteenth century engineering achievement awards. In a place where scattered scrub trees were the primary source of wood, miners and their crews built intricate mazes of elevated sluices, working streams that were barely visible among the huge gravel spoil piles and meandering woodworks.

When writing about the Klondike, most historians and authors focus on the "rush of 1898." The story has been retold dozens of times, testament to our fascination with this incredible example of human determination, where mere survival often could be as unlikely as staking a successful claim. Yet northern mining history began long before the gold rush. For decades, a handful of miners, most fitting the stereotypical mold of grizzled, lonely men, wandered Western Canada from British Columbia and the Yukon Territory north and west to the Alaska Territory. Many were old California forty-niners still searching for their fortune, still content to be looking even when gold never materialized. From the 1850s until the mid-1890s little changed in the "land of the Esquimaux" and the rest of the world continued to ignore this unknown land.

But when word of northern treasures reached Seattle in the summer of 1897, Klondike life changed dramatically. While the gold rush is an epic tale of determination, the making of Klondike society is equally remarkable--a phenomenon that began before most had even planned their journey north. Gold had been discovered nearly a year earlier, in August 1896, and by the time word filtered to the Outside and the rush began the following summer, most of the richest claims along Bonanza and Eldorado creeks in the Klondike mining district had been staked.

By 1898, Dawson City and Grand Forks were an odd mixture of tent hotels, restaurants and rapidly rising boom-town contruction. The emerging society was a cross-section of humanity--scheming businessmen, devout clergy, prim and proper school teachers, brazen prostitutes, quiet families and hardworking men who slaved round-the-clock in the mines and celebrated even harder when the spring cleanup was complete.

As the boom transformed tent towns into bustling communities, an estimated 25,000 people called Dawson City home, and another

Above--Clarke Kinsey, shown here, devoted more time to photography than mining, even though he and his brother Clarence owned several family claims. Most surviving photos show the younger Clarke with clean clothes and a broad grin, Clarence with the telltale mud-encrusted miner's boots.

Right--No amount of ingenuity could change the elements in this inhospitable land. Both the size of the crew and the days, weeks and months of hard work in winter determined the amount of gravel that could be poured through the sluices when the spring thaw came.

9

10,000 were ensconsed in and around the little town of Grand Forks, at the intersection of Bonanza and Eldorado creeks. Dawson, the largest city north and west of Victoria and Winnipeg, Canada, was a metropolis in turn-of-the-century terms, while Grand Forks was the smaller, blue-collar community.

Hourly laborers, well-dressed claim owners and their wives present a cross-section of Klondike society as they gather around a sluice box at 28-Above-Bonanza. The Kinsey caption calls this a record cleanup of $52,000. (Whether this was a record to date for claims Above-Bonanza, for the season or for the creek is unclear.)

Nevada ✦ Restaurant ✦ and ✦ Cafe ✦

Monday Feby 24th 1896

DINNER BILL OF FARE

SIDE ORDER OYSTERS 25 CENTS EXTRA

SOUP
Puree of Split Pea, au Croutons
Chiffonade Julienne

FISH
Fish Chowder with Rice
Shrimp Salad.   Newfoundland Style

BOILED
1888 Ham. Sauce Robert.

ENTREES
Civett of Chicken au Petit Pois
Calves Heart. a l' Jardinien
Liver Brochettes Brown Gravy.
Italian Fritters Lemon Sauce.

ROASTS
Leg of Young Pork with Apple Sauce
Prime Ribs of Beef au Jus.

VEGETABLES
Green Peas   Stewed Carrots
Boiled and Mashed Potatoes

DESSERT
Assorted Cakes
Oregon and Edam Cheese.
Mixed Nuts and Raisins.

PIES   **PUDDING**
Hot Mince   *Corn Starch*
Peach.   *Vanilla Sauce*

EXTRAS
1/2 Broiled Spring Chicken 75
Fresh Eastern Oysters any Style 50
Pickled Pigs Feet 35. Salmon Bellies 35
1/2 Ptarmigan 45. Whole Ptarmigan 65.

EASTERN OYSTERS ANY STYLE 50 CENTS
WINE LIST ON THE OTHER SIDE

LUNCH FROM 11 A. M. TO 2 P. M. 50 CENTS

DINNER FROM 4 TO 9 P. M. 50 CENTS

Courtesy of Jim Johnson

Liquor shortages and exorbitant prices were legendary during the rush and first years of settlement in the Klondike, but fresh food was always in demand and worth whatever price it could fetch. James Johnson's Nevada Restaurant and Cafe was a mountain pass stop for many a gourmet en route to the Klondike. Johnson later moved on to Dawson City, where he operated the Dawson Flume Hose Factory.

11

12

This early photograph of a Grand Forks-area panorama is rare. Virtually all of the surviving city photographs were taken between 1900 and 1904 when Grand Forks was a thriving little town of nearly 10,000 people. This view from Eldorado toward Dawson City was probably taken around 1898. The photograph is part of the Ronald Kinsey collection, but was reproduced from a print rather than a surviving glass plate negative.

CX905. Panoramic view of No. 16 Eldorado— where Millionaire Lippy of Seattle reaped his harvest of gold—Y. T.

The End of the Rainbow

The Newcomer In Dawson

There are many men in Dawson at the present time who feel keenly disappointed. They have come thousands of miles on a perilous trip, risked life, health and property, spent months of the most arduous labor a man can perform, and with expectations raised to the highest pitch, have reached the coveted goal only to discover the fact that there is nothing here for them.

Any man of ordinary judgement might well have reached the conclusion long before he set out for Dawson that every creek and gulch

One of the first, and richest, Klondike claims was the famous Number 16 Eldorado, where Seattle's Tom Lippy became a millionaire before most stampeders had even begun their journey north.

adjacent to the city would be staked months before he could possibly reach it. The gold is here beyond question and should anyone have thoughts of becoming suddenly wealthy without any considerable exertion on his own part he will fail in nine cases out of ten. On the other hand if he brings with him a due amount of pluck and energy and a willingness to endure hardship and privation, in the long run the chances are favorable for his success.

The Klondike Nugget
June 23, 1898

"Considerable exertion" and "privation" were polite words of forewarning for the men who held fast to hopes of finding gold. Virtually all of the claims on Bonanza and Eldorado creeks were staked by the time this June 1898 article was published. But as *The Klondike Nugget* reported, there were still new creeks to discover, claims to be filed and good profits--if not fortunes--to be made. Surrounding creeks--Hunker, Dominion, Gold Bottom and others--and hillside claims provided the justification many miners needed to stay a summer or a decade. The economy on the Outside was failing, and many had come from the West Coast, where business was mired in a depression.

However, those who found wealth after 1898 were not only lucky or hardworking miners. They were, for the most part, entrepreneurs and businessmen and women who bought and sold claims, shipped goods, ran stores and hotels and brought good business sense to the Klondike society. Changes in everything from lifestyles to prices came quickly.

The *Nugget* reported, ". . . flour that once sold for $75 per sack dropped in December to $50; in February it could be bought for $40, in March for $30, and the latest reports (April) are that it may be had for $10."

Miners lean against an ore car before it is hauled up to the top of the sluices, where the gravel will be washed out.

But more often, prices remained high: whiskey brought $40 to $50 per gallon; wine, $75 to $100; and straight alcohol, $80.

Inflated prices were not the only obstacles the new society had to overcome. The Klondike was hardly the Eldorado so many had expected and the hope of finding gold was often more sustaining than gold itself in the face of harsh winters and dreadful conditions. Tents often had to suffice for first-winter quarters and health standards were deplorable.

Sewage and garbage quickly became unmanageable, and when the spring thaw came, the stench around the creeks could be overpowering. In Dawson sewage drained into surrounding swamps,

This photograph, captioned by the Kinseys only as "Roberts (holding the fork) and Bill Finn (to his left)," keenly depicts the tools and other paraphernalia used in early Klondike mining. The men are surrounded by riffles, narrow slats which will be fitted into the bottom of sluices to catch the larger gravel and rocks. Note the tailing piles in the background which are left after the gold has been washed from the dirt.

threatening newly arrived prospectors with malaria, typhoid and dysentery. Fortunately, a Jesuit missionary from Alaska, Father William Judge, had already begun plans to build a hospital in 1897. But the hastily-constructed building which resulted could not begin to accommodate the number of settlers who streamed to the doors with scurvy and other diseases. Father Judge himself died of pneumonia and overwork in January of 1899.

The clergy established churches quickly, but their preachings could not compete for the majority of the miners' attention; for every house of worship, there were a dozen houses of ill-repute. Miners did not even have to cross town to the prostitutes' cabins to spend their money. More than a handful of miners lost every penny they had earned to the dance hall girls in the saloons. The women had no trouble conning them out of cash or selling them time, either for a dance in the saloon or a trip to the rooms above the bar.

Miners were not the only members of Klondike society whose earthly thoughts outweighed religious devotion. In an 1898 letter responding to a plea from a Grand Forks minister, a local official wrote:

> I intend shortly to make a tour of all the gold creeks and will pay particular attention to this matter of Sunday labour. I firmly believe from a Utilitarian point of view only that it would be advantageous for the Sunday Observance Act to be strictly enforced. Men work better if they have a rest on the seventh day.

But despite the fact that attention often focused on gold instead of God, churches flourished across the street or down the block from saloons. Many sought solace at makeshift altars or escaped from the harsh mining life to pray in shipping crate pews.

The Bonanza Detachment of the North West Mounted Police was headquartered across the dirt street from "the row," which housed the prostitutes of Grand Forks. This kind of order in the midst of chaos characterized Klondike life and provided the foundation for the growing society.

Clergymen and congregation members gather for services at
Dominion Creek outside Grand Forks.

During the early years of the Klondike, clergymen established churches, such as the Presbyterian Church of Grand Forks shown here, in log cabins, tents or any makeshift structure that would keep out the wind and weather. Within a short time, however, three large, steepled churches were erected to accommodate devoted townspeople.

NO 4 BELOW ON BONANZA

KINSEY&KINSEY PHOTO

This Bonanza mine is a prime example of Klondike engineering--
a boiler house for pumping sluice water and thawing frozen overburden and a narrow-gauge bucket-and-rail system for hauling
gold-bearing gravel. Even as mining became mechanized, some
crews still had to settle for tents in lieu of cabins. Comfort always
22   took a back seat to potential profits.

Left--An old-timer shows a young miner the art of using a rocker box, which sifted out fine sand and dirt and left the gold behind.

Below--The "jiger" being operated is a hand jigger--or rocker box. The logged-out hillside in the background is typical of landscapes in the Klondike, where every tree, regardless of size, was needed for sluices.

This photograph was probably taken to portray friends, rather than to document a newsworthy event of the era. However, that element of the Kinsey photography--a more personal rather than a strictly journalistic approach--is invaluable in allowing us to paint a true portrait of the Klondiker. Like so many Kinsey glass plate negatives, this image barely survived the trip Outside.

This elevated sluiceway *(right)* was located on a Hunker Creek mine, a gold-bearing, but less profitable creek than either the famous Eldorado or Bonanza. James Johnson, the proprietor of the Nevada Restaurant and Cafe, paid $15 for a permit to mine a claim on Hunker in 1901 *(below)*.

Grant for Placer Mining.

DEPARTMENT OF THE INTERIOR,

Agency,_____ 189___

In Consideration of the payment of Fifteen Dollars, being the fee prescribed by clause 28 of the Mining Regulations for the Yukon District by *J H Johnson*, of DAWSON Y T accompanying *his* application No. *65933* dated *May 2nd* 190 for a Mining Claim in *Hunker*

Mining Division of the Dawson District

The Minister of the Interior hereby grants to the said *J H Johnson* for the term of one year from the date hereof the exclusive right of entry upon the claim *Hillside adjoining the lower half of Right Limit of No 40 below Discovery on Hunker Creek Loc apl 30190 YMC*

for the miner-like working thereof and the construction of a residence thereon, and the exclusive right to all the proceeds realized therefrom, upon which, however, the royalty prescribed by the Regulations shall be paid.

The said *J H Johnson* shall be entitled to the use of so much of the water naturally flowing through or past *said* claim, and not already lawfully appropriated, as shall be necessary for the due working thereof, and to drain *said* claim free of charge.

This Grant does not convey to the said *J H Johnson* any right of ownership in the soil covered by the said claim ; and the said grant shall lapse and be forfeited unless the claim is continuously and in good faith worked by the said *J H Johnson* or *his* associates.

The rights hereby granted are those laid down in the aforesaid Mining Regulations, and no more, and are subject to all the provisions of the said Regulations, whether the same are expressed herein or not.

Mining Recorder.

Courtesy of Jim Johnson

During the early winters mining was a grueling process only accomplished with heavy labor and bonfires to melt the frozen earth. Yet even the women donned miner's boots during sub-zero temperatures. Steam pipes and pumps quickly replaced bonfires and were usually powered by small boilers.

Condition of the Streets

Dawson is unfortunate in her streets. Teams and wagons have appeared this summer and things are in worse condition than ever before. Ladies can be seen at the north end of town, where there are no sidewalks, who actually have to stop once in a while at some convenient pool and wash the clinging mud from their footwear. Mud, mud, everywhere, and were it not for the eternal frost beneath, it would be bottomless. As it is, the hubs of the wheals [sic] guage [sic] the depths of the mud and the axle-trees drag as they did in Chicago in the early days. The summer season is short and a few loads of sawdust would soon make the main street clean and passable.

The Klondike Nugget
July 2, 1898

PERCENTAGE AVENUE. GRAN

"Percentage Avenue" was probably an early name for this rough stretch of springtime quagmire. The Canadian government surveyed and platted the community of Grand Forks after the land was already staked and settled and many original street names gave way to numbers and government-given titles.

Road to the Forks

Every mine owner, every layman and in fact every miner on the creeks is loud in his demand for a good double wagon road to at least Grand Forks, and everybody is wondering why it is that the Yukon council has not long ago taken some heroic measure to meet this crying need so essential to the development of the country.

The lack of such a road has already created losses far in excess of the original costs of such a road, not alone to the miners, but to the government itself. A large number of the dumps which have been put out on Bonanza, and Eldorado especially, will not be washed out this summer, while a larger proportion of the gravel put out on the hillsides and benches will not be cleaned up for the reason of the great shortage of the supply of water.

A number of the larger operators who had prepared to work their claims this summer on benches and hillsides, will not be able to do so to as great an extent as intended or expected, for the reason that they were unable to have hauled to their claims the machinery necessary for pumping the water. Most of the large dumps already put out and which will not be washed this summer would have been sluiced had the owners been able to have had the necessary machinery hauled to their claims.

The failure in every such instance is due to the lack of a good, serviceable wagon road from Dawson to the Forks. When the millions of dollars involved in the matter are considered, both to owners, miners and government, it seems almost criminal on the part of the government to evade the issue by a technical excuse for failing to do what should have been done two years ago.

It is understood that just at present the Yukon Council is powerless to act because it has no funds at its disposal for that purpose. While this may be so now it was not the case a year ago, especially when the amount necessary as compared to importance is so very small.

An expenditure of certainly not more than $20,000 would give a good road to the Forks. This would mean much to everybody interested in mining on the creeks, from the highest to the lowest. It would cause a reduction of fully 50 percent in the present rate of freight charges, which under existing conditions are fairly moderate and this reduction would mean a saving to the miners of say $60,000 on every thousand tons taken to the Forks. More than that it would cause an increase in the output of gold during the summer months. Those total would be enough to pay the cost of the road, and probably pay for more than twice over out of the royalties that would be collected by the government.

Dawson Daily News
June 20, 1900

Passengers on the Orr & Tukey stageline stop at a Bonanza Creek roadhouse. Orr & Tukey was one of the largest and most successful passenger and freight stagelines in the Klondike, hauling an average of four to eight tons of goods per freight run between Dawson and Grand Forks, and as many passengers as the stage could hold.

Klondike miner George Archer *(far left)*, Clarence
Kinsey and miner-artist Asa Thurston Hayden
strike jaunty poses for the photographer. Hayden
was relatively talented at a form of copper or
wood etching; while none of the original artwork
survives, much of it--accompanied by original or
borrowed poetry--was documented on the
Kinseys' glass plates *(see opposite photo)*.

WE LIV'D ON THE GAME WHICH OUR RIFLES SHOT, EXPLORING THE COUNTRY 'ROUND,
AND CAMP'D IN A SHELTER OF BRUSH AND LOGS WHEN WE REACH'D THE HUNTING GROUND

Tents remained commonplace long after cities were well-established. This tent served as the No. 30 store where miners could get a hot meal, catch a freight to Dawson or buy wine, liquor and cigars. Ed Kinsey, a brother who came north to share the excitement of the Klondike with Clarke and Clarence, apparently found his calling as a cook. He is on the left in the apron and towel hat.

Deaths at the Hospital

Below we give the deaths which have occurred at the hospital since it was opened, August 20, 1897. Considering the fact that since that time 275 patients have been occupants, the death rate has been amazingly low:

Fred Hart..Philadelphia
Andrew Johnson.....................................Odd Fellows buried
Paul Meug..Switzerland
John Parker..Portland
John A. Lauglois..Canada
Peter Shearer..Tacoma
Jas. S. Cooper...New York (Tacoma)
H.H. McQuillin..Chicago
J.M. Stacey..Tacoma
John Silva..(Italian)
Thos. Harvey...Victoria
Nels Oleson...................................(Thought Tacoma)
John Freedland..Tacoma
Edw. Dustan...Unknown
Capt. Hamlin.............................(On government survey)
Wm. McKillop.......................................(Scotchman)
Theo. Walentine (sailor)...............................Norway
Andrew Skinrud.....................................Wiota, Iowa
Andrew Nelson...Unknown
N.P. Swanson...Unknown
John Galvin..Juneau
Wm. S. Myers..Unknown
Wm. J. Law..Old Mexico
David Roebig..Unknown
Gus Anderson..Unknown

The Klondike Nugget
June 16, 1898

The Kinseys reveled in photographic storytelling. Unfortunately, the faces in this typical mining portrait have no names to accompany them. However, the photographer summed up the scene of men and women in suits and furs beside sluiceways running with spring water, but no gold, by etching his own commentary on the negative--"Skunked."

Downtown Grand Forks may have looked shabby during its heyday with its clapboard storefronts, muddy streets and flimsy boardwalks, but the town was thriving nevertheless. Millions of dollars worth of goods and gold rolled through the streets to and from Dawson. Stage and freight lines generated much of their business travelling the fourteen-mile stretch of rutted permafrost between Dawson and Grand Forks and out along the adjacent creeks. This ten-mule freight team likely was hauling mining supplies from Dawson.

39

N.W.M POLICE
DETACHMENT GRAND FORKS Y.T.

Caretakers of the North

Dawson, Dec. 11, 1899

Sir:

I have the honour to transmit herewith a return showing the number of miles travelled by the members of the N.W.M.Police during the months of December, January, February, March and April last while employed in carrying the mail....The total mileage travelled is as follows:

B. Division........20,965
H. Division........43,047
Total   64,012

The Bonanza Detachment of the North West Mounted Police, first citizens of Grand Forks, pose in front of their barracks.

List of Lunatics confined in Dawson Gaol during month of Feby. – 1901.

Name		Date of arrest	Date of committal	By whom	Crime	Nationality	No. of days confined	Remarks
Schlicht	Ellerslie	Dec. 6/00	Dec. 27/00	Insp McDonell		Am.	84	Very noisy at intervals during day & night.
Watson	Edw.	Jany. 5/01				Am.	6	Released fit to be at large. 2nd Confinement
Hout	Louis	" 31/01	Feby. 12	" "		Am.	29	Violent from 1st to 4th, broke door of cell is now tractable
Reid	Jno.	Feby. 3	" 12	" "		Br.	26	Violent from 3rd to 6th, since then more subdued.
Miller	Thro.	" 12	" 21	" "		Am.	17	Very noisy at intervals day & night.
Fogarty	B.B.	May 27/00	June 6/00	Supt Primrose	Theft	Am.	268	Sentenced to one year H.L., quiet & melancholly.

Few prisoners can get used to the irritating clamour of a number of Lunatics, it is annoying during the day and almost unbearable night after night to be awakened by the noise, there is now much discussion as to the treatment of these insane patients, but in the name of humanity could not a little sympathy be enlisted for prisoners who day after day and year after year have been compelled to listen to the almost incessant babblings of a number of Lunatics; it is almost more than nature can be expected to stand.

Copy.

(Sgd.) Geo. H. Tweedy
Provost. S/Sergt.

Often those who were deemed insane and confined to Klondike prisons by the North West Mounted Police were suffering more from loneliness and poor physical health than any real mental disorder. Yet the so-called mentally insane were viewed just as, if not more, onerous than common criminals. As the comments in this record reveal, "lunatics" and lawbreakers were jailed in the same building, much to the dismay of Sgt. Tweedy and the other prisoners.

As the duty of carrying the mail entailed a great amount of hardship upon the members of the Force which could not be contemplated in their original engagement as members of the Force, I recommend that extra pay be allowed to all who were thus employed.

It seems to me the mileage basis is the fairest way of arriving at the distribution of any amount which may be granted for this purpose. I strongly recommend that 15 cents a mile be allowed. The total amount would reach $9,601.80. A large amount of additional work was thrown upon Officers and many others who under the mileage scale will not receive compensation. However, I cannot see any other way of arriving at the duty thus performed. I trust that you will approve my recommendation and that early payment may be made.

Letter to the Comptroller, North West Mounted Police, from the Superintendent, Dawson City, Y.T.

As this letter reveals, the North West Mounted Police performed many duties outside the conventional realm of law enforcement. The Mounties were not just policemen, but care-takers of order: they delivered the mail, collected the taxes, settled domestic disputes, built public buildings and even determined who was sane or insane upon the request of the federal government.

But the Mounties' efforts did not go unnoticed. They were admired and respected throughout the Klondike. Even the miners, generally acknowledged as the most unruly members of society, seemed to respect their presence and the need for lawfulness. In his account of police service during the gold rush years, Non-Commissioned Officer M.H.E. Hayne reflected, "We made occasional patrols around the principal creeks at which mining was going on, but whether it was that the men were really a peaceable, orderly lot, or whether the mere knowledge of our presence and the fact that we held supreme power acted as a healthy restraint, I do not know. Probably there was a little of both."

The typical occupants of the jailhouse were relatively harmless, considering the rapid growth and haphazard makeup of the population--vagrants or drunks in for an overnight stay, or by one account, a lonely miner from Europe who could not speak English found wandering aimlessly. The unfortunate foreigner, his confused responses interpreted as deranged babblings, was locked up for months, labeled insane by the local sergeant.

According to the Kinseys' caption, these men are returning to Dawson or Grand Forks from a stampede. From the looks of their calm and unhurried expressions, the rumors of gold which led them to some distant creek or field proved untrue.

AFTER THE SPRING CLEAN UP.

KINSEY & KINSEY.

As the ornaments on the tree at left suggest, miners never failed to reward their own efforts with alcohol. Liquor was expensive, but it flowed like spring runoff once the cleanup was complete. The woman in the right foreground was likely a claim owner and shared in the celebration alongside her partners and employees.

In the Police Court

In the police court today H.F. Berge was bound over to keep the peace and remanded to jail until such time as he could secure sufficient sureties for his good behavior. He was arrested for threatening to kill his wife, who has become fearful for her life and appealed to the police for protection. Her sister, Augusta Waechter, testified concerning Berge's cruel treatment and neglect of his wife. The couple were married in Dawson in December and later on opened a road house at Indian River. Recently it was destroyed by fire. Since then they have lived in town, and the husband has been idle and carousing about the saloons.

Dawson Daily News
February 22, 1900

As high food prices made headlines, many miners hunted duck, pheasant or other game for food. Rifles and shotguns were vital in putting meat on the table, but sidearms were virtually nonexistent in the Klondike--illegal by Canadian law and typically confiscated by the North West Mounted Police. Sidearms that did find their way there played a larger role in suicides than in murders or robberies.

The Grand Hotel in downtown Grand Forks, still referred to as Bonanza on this 1902 Kinsey glass plate, was just one site of celebration during Canadian Dominion Day. Members of the North West Mounted Police, a ubiquitous presence in the Klondike, stand among the crowd. Clarence Kinsey is standing at the left, just behind the horse.

About Dawson's Post Office

Rapid Increase in the Quantity of
Mail Received

. . . The mounted police department was drafted into the service with immediately beneficial results. Police posts are being or already have been established every fifty miles from salt water on Pyramid Harbor to Dawson City and every police post is a post office and every policeman a possible postman if his services should be so required. The improvement was immediate and commendable and on the first of the year the mails commenced to roll into Dawson. . . .

The great trouble now seems to be this accumulation of mail matter. Only a fraction of the letters arriving are delivered within a month, and thousands are never delivered at all. The result is an aggravating slow delivery and a long line of inquiries is found at the office from early morning till night. The weary waiters stand out in the mud and rain reclining on boxes, boards and blocks, in every attitude of distress until it becomes a crying shame.

Inspector Harper, Dawson's gentlemanly post master, is looking for tenders till noon Wednesday for a new post office building, twenty by thirty feet. In this new office are to be placed boxes for those getting large quantities of mail, and pigeon-holes will be multiplied, until names can be divided, even to the third letter. Letters not delivered within a specified time will be stored away or sent back to the dead letter office. Mr. Harper believes that these improvements will enable Dawsonites to get their mail without delay hereafter.

The Klondike Nugget
July 5, 1898

mr. Downing. with His Team. U.S. mail Carrier.

Kinsey & Kinsey

Fortunately, the North West Mounted Police were relieved of their postal service duties around the turn of the century. In this 1902 photograph U.S. Mail Carrier Mr. Downing is pictured with his team in front of the Yukon Territorial Administration Building in Dawson. In his duties as mailman, he carried letters from Dawson to Nome on their way Outside, mushing the breadth of Alaska and back again.

The Dog Nuisance

Dogs everywhere, day and night, howling, fighting, filthy, mangy dogs--all these and more form at present one of the worst nuisances that has for a long time afflicted the citizens of Dawson.

This is the season of the year when cruel and selfish owners of dogs, with no further use for them, have turned them loose on the community to prey for an existence. . . .

There are more dogs in town today than there ever were before. It is calculated that there are at least 2,000 dogs now running loose on the streets of Dawson. Fully one-half of them are homeless by reason of their owners following the annual summer custom of driving them away to rustle for themselves with the intention of recovering them in the fall when their services shall again become valuable. Last year the government established a dog pound and passed a dog ordinance which tended to some extent in clearing the streets and sidewalks of the troublesome dogs and their filthy habits.

Unfortunately, however, the dog pound was located east of the town near the foot of the hill in the most thickly populated portion of the hillside, and the result was a howling mass of ill-assorted, half-starved canines that kept the neighborhood awake every night and drove many people to the verge of insanity.

Dawson Daily News
May 23, 1900

Despite the negative commentary in the *Dawson Daily News*, dogs played a vital role in the Klondike--as sled and pack animals at the height of the rush and as companions for lonely miners in those early years. They often meant the difference between life and death during the winter. Good, strong sled dogs could sell for several hundred dollars when miners were desperate to reach the claims and a smart would-be miner would feed the animals the best food first, saving beans and dried goods for himself. Once in the Klondike, the animals were valuable beasts of burden in the winter, but often regarded as nuisances in spring and summer.

Grand Forks; Bonanza, Y.T.

This snow-and-slush view of Grand Forks illustrates the town's impermanence, even as the gold rush approached its peak. Coutts Stable, a major Grand Forks business, was housed in a large tent. Just above the Coutts sign is Woodburn's drugstore. Along First Avenue to the right of Woodburn Drugs was hotel row--the Grand Forks Hotel, the Northern and the Dewey, and just beyond was the North West Mounted Police headquarters.

53

Growing Up

"**M**y parents bought a store in Grand Forks and named it the Bonanza Clothing Store. My father had a cardroom in the back of the store where the miners used to play 'frog solo.'

"I acquired a three-dog team and a good sleigh and hauled water in the winter, from 21-Above-on-Bonanza and sold it for twenty-five cents for four gallons. We had two small barrels on the sleigh and once they were filled, we dipped flour sacks into the water and placed them over the barrels with hoops--they froze in

Young miners, many still in their teens, were a common sight in the Klondike. This miner has loaded all of his belongings, including a table and wash tubs, on pack horses.

Even water was a scarce commodity in the Klondike when the winter freeze came, sometimes lasting as long as eight months. When temperatures dropped very low, water delivery was halted altogether and families had to dig up snow, despite the layer of soot on top, and boil and strain it for cooking and drinking.

a minute and we never lost a drop of water. I also used the dogs to go up to Bonanza and Eldorado creeks, selling papers and magazines.

"I drove a two-horse stage from Grand Forks to Quartz Creek on Sundays and got four dollars doing this--I was only 11 years old then. . . . I remember a chap who brought a load of eggs over the trail from Whitehorse in a covered sleigh. He had lanterns burning inside the sleigh, but in spite of the lanterns, some of the eggs froze. I had the job of candelling some of them for the N. & T. Co. The frozen eggs were used to mix in dog feed and the good ones sold for $4.25 a dozen."

Jim Kingsley, Sr., remembering his experiences as a boy in Grand Forks

56

Miners work near a shaft on this hillside claim. The miner at left is standing in the sluice, shoveling gravel which was brought up from the shaft throughout the winter.

Blanketed horses, probably recently purchased and used for hauling freight, line the front of Bayless' Kentucky Horse Market in this 1901 photograph. Clarke is on horseback in the striped shirt and Clarence stands to the right of him holding a horse's harness.

One-room schoolhouses dotted the Klondike. The Yukon government controlled education, hired teachers and supplied materials--from primers to lumber--for the schoolhouse. The basics of reading, writing and arithmetic were taught in the typical one-room fashion, with students of all ages grouped together.

Inspectors were routinely sent to evaluate the progress of the students, and report on more practical matters such as the sturdiness of the schoolhouse or regularity of wood delivery. John McKay taught the pupils at the Grand Forks school in its first years, but received less than glowing recommendations when the territorial inspector visited. In his review to the commissioner, John Ross wrote:

> He is fully capable of teaching, but does not appear to take much interest in his work...there are twenty-one pupils and there were seventeen present. It was impossible for me to judge them as far as their progress was concerned because only five of those who were there before [on my last visit] were in attendance that day.
>
> There are eight large boys in this (fourth) class and one girl and they have only attended during the months of March and April.
>
> In the infant class there were two little boys that had only mastered a few of the sounds of the letters and only knew number work up to the number four. They were both less than six years old.

The school building is situated in a rather low place and there is no playground around it at this time of year. It is also in great need of suitable seats and until these are obtained it will be impossible for good work to be done in the school.

Such was education in the Klondike, where living from one day to the next was more urgent than providing children with a formal elementary school education. Harsh weather often made it impossible to get to school and families moved frequently in search of more profitable settlements or gold-bearing ground. A miner might live in Dawson one season and move to Grand Forks--or Hunker or Dominion--the next. And school-age children were often too valuable working in a family business or mine to be allowed to attend school consistently.

Young schoolchildren surround their teacher outside a one-room schoolhouse, which bears the sign, "All Welcome."

Above--Although bleak winter conditions often prevented
children from coming to school, this Yukon class portrait shows
healthy attendance despite the snow and ice.

Opposite--The blueprints shown here were drawn for the Bonanza
School at Grand Forks. Before plans for the new building were
drawn and carried out, a local church was used as a schoolroom;
because the teacher had to stand far above the class on a platform
which once served as the altar and the children were sitting in "old
fashioned church seats," the building was pronounced unsuitable.

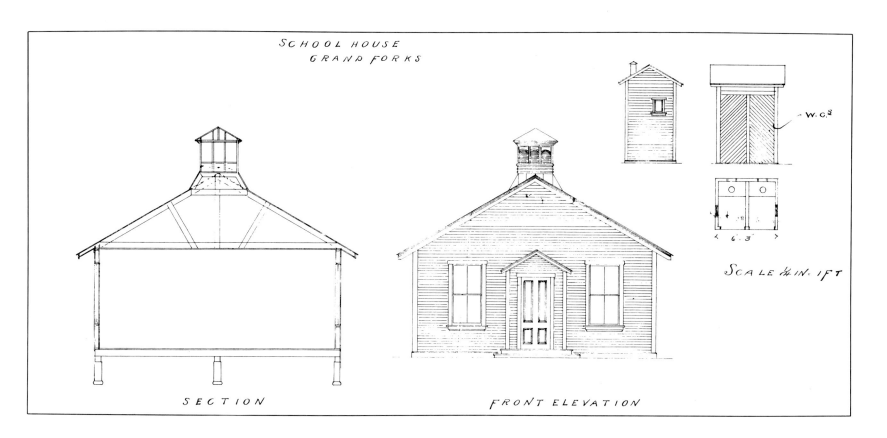

SCHOOL HOUSE
GRAND FORKS

W.C.s

SCALE ¼ IN = 1 FT

SECTION

FRONT ELEVATION

6.3

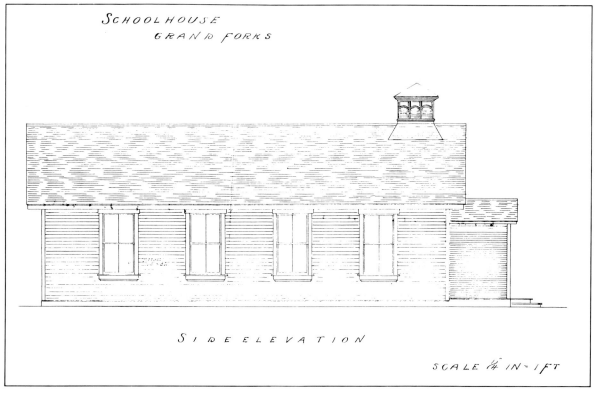

SCHOOL HOUSE
GRAND FORKS

SIDE ELEVATION

SCALE ¼ IN = 1 FT

63

The government attempted to organize Grand Forks, which had
been staked and claimed haphazardly during the early years of the
gold rush. Titles to cabin and store lots had to be reclaimed, streets
adjusted and the original Bonanza townsite replatted.

NOTICE !

Notice is hereby given that the Lot on which this Cabin is built is now open for sale.

The owner of the Cabin has the first privilege of purchasing the Lot on which it is built, by paying the full purchase price not later than the 1st day May, 1902, at my office, otherwise on that date all improvements on said Lot will be deemed abandoned by owner and confiscated to the Crown, and will become the property of the first applicant to purchase said Lot whose application may be approved. This Notice is final.

F. X. GOSSELIN,

Dawson, February 22, 1902.   Crown Timber and Land Agent.

The Grand Forks branch of the Dawson Transfer stageline offered one-way passage to Dawson for $2 and a round-trip ticket for $3.50. The company was originally owned by H. H. Honnen, who sold the business to open a mining company.

TIME TABLE

Dawson Transfer Co.'s
STAGES

Leave Dawson for Bonanza and Eldorado 9 a.m. and 6 p.m.

Leave Bonanza for Dawson at 8 a.m. and 6 p.m.

Leave Dawson for Hunker and Gold Bottom 5 p. m.

Gold Bottom for Dawson 8 a.m.

TELEPHONE NO. 6

Office: Opposite N. C. Building,

Where Strong Men Turn Back

Where Strong Men Turn Back Before Hardships, Brave Women Continue the Journey

In the rush of thousands who started for the Klondike in '97, history will never record the number of strong men who paled before the dangerous hardships and the many vicissitudes enroute, and returned to their homes determined to wander no more. Does anyone know of a woman who grew faint-hearted and turned back of her own accord?

If you have an aversion for the "new woman," a week on the Dyea trail would change that aversion to admiration, for there you may see

In addition to their household duties, women often worked alongside their husbands on small claims, pushing wheel-barrows or panning fine gold from sluices.

Miners' wives and children stand by their claim, taking a break from the long, spring day's work.

big, husky husbands and brothers discouraged and faint-hearted preparing to return to the comforts of their homes, while the brave little wife or sister begs with tears in her eyes to continue the journey.

Miss B. Mulrooney, the subject of this sketch, had no big brother or husband to rely upon, but she believed that if a woman could grace almost any business or profession at home she could be a successful trail blazer.

She fitted out in Seattle in '97, and started alone to Dyea, which place she reached on April 1st. Here she joined a party of prominent mining men and made the trip to Lake Bennett, and in a large scow started for the mines. She kept the party supplied with fish and meat by the aid of gun and rod, in the handling of which she is an expert. She staked out claim 22 below on Henderson, a location which is destined to have mining in the near future.

On June 10th, she arrived in Klondike City with a 2,000 pound outfit and only twenty-five cents in money. She threw the coin far out into the swift water of the Yukon "just for luck," as she expressed it.

A few weeks after her arrival in Dawson, she was again in the restaurant business. She charged from $1.50 to $4.50 for a meal, until the panic cry was raised and provisions went up to $2 a pound. She then built a two-story hotel at the forks of Eldorado and Bonanza and named the town site "Grand Forks," where she now does a thriving trade.

The Klondike News
April 1, 1898

Belinda Mulrooney poses in all of her finery with her husband, Charles Eugene Carbonneau, who arrived in Dawson selling champagne and claiming to be a French count. Although he was later identified as a barber from Montreal, the couple still journeyed to Paris for their honeymoon.

Belinda Mulrooney was perhaps the most successful woman entrepreneur in the Klondike, and was in fact the first person to establish a permanent business at Grand Forks. Whether she named the townsite is suspect, but she did name her establishment the Grand Forks Hotel. The townsite was known as Bonanza for many years before the Canadian government officially renamed it. Many stories of Belinda's cunning and business talents have become Klondike legend. Her assets included the Grand Forks Hotel, several successful claims (most of which she was reputed to have acquired with a keen ear and quick financial reaction), and later the finest hotel in the Klondike, The Fairview. It overlooked the Yukon in Dawson City and few disputed that it was the most elegant hotel in the territory at the time of its construction.

Miss M. Gates was also known for her spirit of enterprise and adventure. The *Dawson Daily News* reported that "Miss Gates has all the sagacity and pluck of a successful financier or a bold mining speculator. In the spring of 1898 she was one of the first parties to arrive in Dawson from Eureka, California....[During her journey] she seemed never to tire nor ever to lose sight of the importance of holding on to the trail as long as dogs and men could stand up to the mushing." In addition to her own valuable bench and hillside claims on Eldorado and Bonanza, Miss Gates managed the mines of her brother, well-known entrepreneur Humboldt Gates, during his absence.

While adventure and opportunity drew these enterprising women to the Klondike, their fame was unusual. Women were outnumbered sometimes fifteen to one in the Klondike, and the vast majority of this female population were dance hall girls or prostitutes. Many of these women also owned interest in claims, but their profits from mining usually never compared with what they earned in the saloons or on the row.

Other women worked alongside their husbands at small claims and raised their families. They ran roadhouses or laundries, serving the endless stream of miners who flowed in and out. The wives and mothers fought to maintain a normal family life and orderly household in the midst of the unwelcoming environment.

"The Yukon was no place for a woman with a baby, especially in the winter," Jim Kingsley remembered. "I have seen it seventy-four below-- you couldn't take a dog or horse out in the open otherwise their lungs froze. You can imagine having to cook for the family as well as bathing a baby under those conditions."

But despite the severe conditions, the women faithfully continued to care for their families and their lives often mirrored the routine of pre-Klondike days.

The Kinsey brothers took countless photographs of their own families. Here, Clarence's wife, Agnes *(left)*, and Clarke's wife, Mary, pose for the camera with the serene expressions of well-practiced subjects.

KINSEY&KINSEY PHOTO BONANZA Y.T.

Hotel guests congregate outside of the Royal Hotel No. 7. Typical of Klondike roadhouses and inns, one of the proprietors was a woman.

Photo by Killom

The Entre Nous Gun and Camera Club was just one of the many organizations established by women in the Klondike. As the twofold purpose of the club reveals, women cultivated their interests freely and any pastime was a good excuse to seek the company of other females in a society dominated by men.

The owner of this roadhouse (circa 1904) evidently attempted to soften the appearance of the imposing log structure with lace curtains inside. Because no adjacent structures can be seen, the business was probably located beyond the boundaries of Grand Forks.

She Blew Out Her Brains

Myrtle Brocee Suicides With
"Doc" Richardson's Revolver

Myrtle Brocee committed suicide at midnight Friday, by firing a pistol-ball through the head. Myrtle was occupying a room over Sam Bonneifield's saloon where she has lain sick since some three weeks ago. For a week past she has been convalescent and expected to go to work again at the Tivoli next Monday--she and her sister Florence doing a very neat double turn of singing and dancing.

The pistol used was a 32-calibre Smith & Wesson, the property of Dr. Richardson, who occupied a room diagonally across the hallway from the suicide, and who was out for several hours in the evening, when the weapon was purloined.

Myrtle Brocee is a girl of but 19 years and the story of the struggles which led up to the deed of Friday night make as sad a recitative as any of the many unhappy fates of which Dawson is a witness.

Three weeks ago she found herself weak and nearly delirious with some mysterious fever and called upon Dr. Richardson. He found her in an acute stage of pneumonia with a temperature which rapidly rose to 105 degrees and remained there three days. The thermometers outside showed 45 degrees below zero; her own cabin was frozen up, the hospitals were far away and a chill meant sudden death. H. Woolrich offered the use of his room across the hall, the room in which the dead girl now lies, it was accepted for her and she was put to bed. A nurse was secured, medicines and nourishment were bought and after two weeks of severe illness the patient became convalescent. The occupants of the "loft," as they style the quarters which are the scene of the tragedy, formed a sincere liking for the girl who was such a "good fellow" among them and Woolrich was welcome to bunk with them until his room could be vacated. But, with returning health, came a necessity of work at the theatre, and next Monday night was fixed as the date of her reappearance. That she dreaded it is evidenced by her expressions to friends.

On Friday evening she was called upon by Alex. McFarlane and Mr. Spitzell, who inquired after her health and noticed no unusual depression or elation in her mental condition. She talked of the theatre, of what she was going to sing and sang over the tune for them. She talked of the new dresses she was to have made on the morrow and discussed them as if interested. Picking up her novel she noted the ending and remarked: "Look here! the girl is going to kill herself." Later in the interview she promised to look in on him the following day, remarking: "I'll come in tomorrow and give you a call."

At 10:30 the girl was alone and evidently disrobed. At midnight a number of the occupants of the house heard a muffled shot which was yet so feeble as to fail to provoke investigation. At 2 o'clock the sister, Florence, was on her way home to her rooms at the Melbourne and decided to give her sister a call.

She was accompanied by two prominent citizens who followed her upstairs. Florence opened the door, found the light still burning and glanced at the bed. In a nearly sitting posture, propped up by pillows, habited in a nightdress, and with the bed covers pulled up a little higher than the waist, there rested her sister with blood still apparently running from her temples. With a shriek Florence fled from the room and in an instant all was hubbub and confusion.

Captain Starnes and Corporal Wilson were soon present and Dr. Richardson was aroused from his bed in a twinkling. A touch showed him the girl was dead and cold. A bullet had penetrated the right temple, had passed through the brain and had crashed the skull on the other side, leaving the brains still oozing slowly from the horrible wound. A policeman was placed on guard and the crowd dispersed until the coroner should convene a jury.

James Allan Aikman had known the deceased since she was in Victoria. When she first came to town the deceased had occupied his bed but was absolutely virtuous to the best of his knowledge. When a virtuous woman acted that way he was convinced something was wrong mentally. She told him she had attempted suicide in Victoria and would do it again unless something turned up to rid her of the life she hated and which brought her the importunities of the men. Woolrich might have been sleeping in his own room the last four or five nights. She had neither money nor clothes. "I told her I would not marry her."

The unfortunate girl was laid away as she would have desired had she been a witness of the circumstances. A shapely casket, covered with white cloth, with massive silver plated handles and trimmings held the remains. The interior was upholstered with blue and white silk. The dead girl was habited in a beautifully trimmed dress of white satin with needle-worked ruffles.

White satin shoes adorned the feet which have so often tripped the light fantastic for the amusement of Dawson. The absence of flowers in this land of gloom is painfully apparent. The Rev. Grant read the funeral service where the body had lain in state. The pall bearers were Dr. Richardson, J.A. Aikman, Adolph Spitzell, Charles P. Heath, Alex McFarland and David Fox, Jr. A large number of friends also followed and saw the remains laid away in the grounds overlooking the Klondike.

The Klondike Nugget
December 21, 1898

LARSS & DUCLOS
PHOTOS.
DAWSON.

A GROUP OF HARD WORKERS, DAWSON, Y.T.

No Time for Innocence

"**I** couldn't imagine a better place to be a little girl. It was harsh. But people managed and got along all right. We had canned milk...and never had eggs. Our first altar at the church was made out of two egg crates with a piece across the top.

"My father had the Vendome Hotel in Grand Forks and he had managed the White Horse Hotel in Whitehorse. He never stayed in one place too long...went on to the new strikes.

"When we came to Grand Forks

The photographer wryly captioned this gathering of Dawson's prostitutes, "A Group of Hard Workers," as the women feign wood chopping and other chores in front of their cabins.

we had a cabin, caddy corner from the mounted police barracks and right across the street from the row. I didn't know that the *pretty ladies* were the dance hall girls--the prostitutes. I know my father never wanted those women coming by our house and my mother didn't like me talking to them. But they were always so pretty and they had silk drapes in their windows. I was fascinated by all that silk.

"I remember them writing my mother a note and asking if they could give me a dress. Well, I used to sit on the door with my little brother and sister on my lap helping my mother. And they thought that I was so good doing that so they wanted to give us presents. Oh, I was just a little girl and I never knew who they were.

"We were a happy family."

Ethel Russell Moyer, on her
childhood years in Grand Forks

For children, the Klondike offered endless excitement and adventure. In a quiet Seattle nursing home, more than seventy-five years after her Klondike experience, Ethel Moyer still remembered the thrill of spring cleanup with delight. As a child she was invited with other friends and neighbors to see the wealth that surfaced from some of the richest mines on the creeks and to lend a festive atmosphere to the worksite.

While Ethel remained completely content with the one-room schoolhouse and dirt-floor cabin which had served as a brothel only days before her family's arrival, her parents witnessed the dramatic changes that occurred in the Yukon with the turn of the century. The Klondike had lost its wild and unsettled veneer. Claims were becoming mechanized and crews of dozens-- sometimes hundreds-- worked the ground for absentee owners who pushed to harvest the gold as efficiently and quickly as possible so they could move on to new territory. The frenzied spirit of the gold rush had evaporated, the population was stable and high prices were dropping.

As the Canadian government took more responsibility for the standards of its far-flung territories and the Russells, the Kingsleys and other families and businesspeople worked to build "respectable" communities, the Klondike took on all the trappings of any well-established town or city. But almost as quickly as the telephone lines, boardwalks, passable streets, libraries, men's clubs and society luncheons appeared, the gold began to dwindle.

Although not part of the Kinsey collection and unfortunately uncaptioned, this photograph could well be of the Russells' Vendome Hotel in Grand Forks.

83

January 2, 1905

Hon. Clifford Sifton,
Minister of Interior, Ottawa, Ont.

Sir,

In reference to your telegram of the 23rd December and my reply thereto of the 24th, I beg to submit the following for your information, regarding the presence of "disorderly houses" in Dawson.

Disorderly houses, or what are commonly known as such, do not exist within the boundaries of the city--although there are a few women, single occupants of cabins, who are prostitutes but whose residences are not considered by the Courts as being bawdy houses under the law the women of the "lower world"--that is those that ply their calling as prostitutes openly--are segregated on the South side of the Klondike River, in a suburb of Dawson, known as Klondike City, where they are practically the only inhabitants; they afford no cause of complaint and are not in any way a menace to the morals of the City.

We are however afflicted with an evil much more dangerous to social life, the effects of which are more incidious [sic] and far reaching than open prostitution, and which is rampant in our very midst. I refer to the presence of the so called "dance hall women" who, under the guise of this legalized calling ply their true occupation as prostitutes and flaunt their brazenness openly to the public. During the hours of daylight and early evening they parade the streets, dressed in silks and reeking of perfume and are so conspicuous that they compel the attention of respectable women and children.

From their appearance in such numbers on some of the principal streets of the city, it would appear as if Dawson was infested with prostitutes and that they florished [sic] to an amazing extent. This however is not the case, for the women referred to are the employees of the various dance halls and, while their actual character is well known to the Police, they are removed beyond our jurisdiction and control, because of the fact that their calling is licensed.

Many of these so called dance hall women are prostitutes from the Coast cities, who, perhaps being of preposessing appearance, find it more pleasant and profitable to attach themselves to a dance hall and thus affectually ensure immunity from the interference of the Police. Many of them have rooms near the dance hall in which they belong and entice men to them, after it has been ascertained that they have sufficient money on their persons to make it worthwhile. Cases are continually being brought to our notice in which men have been so enticed, plied with liquor until rendered stupid, and then robbed of their money. Owing to the publicity entailed by an appeal to the Courts, the victims will neither lay information nor volunteer as witnesses, so these women escape punishment.

The dance hall proprietors are prohibited from allowing any person

to occupy any room, or part of his licensed premises, if he "suspects or believes" it is to be used for an improper or immoral purpose, or to allow any female suspected of being a prostitute to occupy any room therein. As the licensee would naturally be the last person in the world to "Believe or suspect" that his patrons, from whom he derives his living have any intention of using his rooms for an immoral or improper purpose, or that the women whom he employs are prostitutes, it is difficult if not impossible to enforce the provisions of the Ordinance. Should any exception be taken to the presence of the women in rooms adjacent to the licensed premises, the licensee can disclaim proprietorship of the rooms as not belonging to or included in his license.

      Sporting women should not be allowed to frequent licensed

This eerie perspective of Dawson's red light district or "White Chapel" at midnight emphasizes the prevalence of prostitution in the Klondike. The Grand Forks "row" was a single column of cabins sandwiched between businesses and residences downtown.

premises, or drink at bars, or on premises in connection therewith, such as boxes, offices or rooms; neither should they be allowed to live over licensed premises, or in rooms over buildings adjoining, when there is connection between such rooms and the licensed premises.

I have the honour to be,
     Sir,
Your obedient servant,

Asst. Commissioner
Comdg. R.N.W.M.Police
Yukon Territory

As the Klondike society became more established, sources of entertainment multiplied. Fraternal organizations and other societies had been formed as early as 1898 and the groups frequently held stage shows, weekend dances and socials.

Above--Smartly attired townspeople crowd beneath the grandstand for a Dominion Day celebration in Grand Forks. *Left*--A small group gathers in front of a cabin at one of Frank and Clarence Berry's rich Eldorado claims.

Well-to-do families shipped more and more luxuries north, until rooms of fine furnishings became indistinguishable from parlors on the Outside. The father of this family even holds a Seattle newspaper on his lap, still another reminder of American homes.

Clarence, Agnes and Olive lived in this elegant and carefully furnished apartment adjoining the back of the Kinseys' photography studio.

Some Little Things

If bric-a-brac is not in any way superior, it is better to group several harmonious pieces, only isolating those to whose fine contour or color you wish to draw attention. The usual three pieces for mantels are, as a rule, too formal for a small room. It is difficult to find anything to add, to break the numerical effect, as these sets are so dignified that to put with them any merely pretty object would produce an incongruity.

While there is a bond between the arts, it is well to give the pictures of musicians a little exclusive corner near the piano, while the other personages, as writers and painters, may be hung in groups or rows near the bookcase. Landscapes should be put together, faces by themselves. This should be done without apparent effort, for evidences of studied effect take away all charms from a room. The success of the hit-or-miss arrangement of pictures is due to its seeming freedom from law.

A good book or magazine is never out of place on a table or tabouret, or in any room. It is often a substitute when a guest is kept waiting for a few minutes.

Dawson Daily News
April 25, 1900

The twentieth century brought various forms of mechanization to mining in the Klondike. Although miners still had to shovel the loose dirt and gravel into the sluices, hydraulic works saved the hand labor of stripping away overburden.

Although a few companies such as the Dawson Flume Hose Factory were launched to accommodate the arrival of hydraulic and other mechanized mining, the economy and ultimate survival of Klondike communities were threatened mainly by industrialization.

When the Dust Had Settled

Mrs. Hall Giving Up the Angelus

Dawson is to lose another one of its pioneer residents. After ten years, Mrs. K. Hall, proprietress of the Angelus on York street, will close the hotel the end of this month and leave for the outside to join her daughter Mrs. Perry, who is now at Los Angeles.

Very popular in Dawson and known by nearly everyone in town, Mrs. Hall has been engaged in the hotel business for many years. At one time she conducted the Brooklyn hotel on Second Avenue. Later she managed the hotel portion

Like many Klondike settlers, the Kinsey brothers ventured west to Alaska when word of gold in Nome spread across the Yukon Territory. But just as quickly as they repainted their sled, adding the word "Nome" in large letters, the Kinseys became unhappy with the town's hectic pace and headed back to Grand Forks. Hundreds of people left Dawson for Nome in 1899, never to return.

of the Principle and about four years ago she opened up the Angelus which was formerly the Idle Hour club.

Before proceeding to Los Angeles, Mrs. Hall intends visiting her mother, Mrs. Christman, the former nurse at Dawson who is now living in retirement at Seattle. Incidentally Mrs. Hall will take in the fair at Seattle.

Dawson Daily News
August 16, 1909

When gold dredges came to the Klondike eight years before this brief item was published, many residents and businesspeople viewed the change as a much-needed boost for the declining population and gold production. In reality, the giant dredges, operated by large conglomerates, sounded the death knell for the Klondike, and hundreds of farewell newspaper articles like this one in the *Dawson Daily News* followed their arrival. The first dredge was no more than a novelty to most of those who watched it in 1901, but by 1906 four machines were in operation with still more to come in a matter of months. What were once stream banks lined by miners' cabins and elaborate boiler, tram and sluiceway operations became acres of symmetrical piles of dirt and gravel discarded by the mammoth dredges.

More and more miners left the Klondike as they saw machinery rip through still gold-bearing strips of land which would have kept them occupied for months. Saloons and dance halls closed, prostitutes looked for other boom towns, businesses were dissolved.

In 1906 the Kinsey & Kinsey partnership came to an end as Clarke, Mary and their two sons left for Seattle, joining the other families who were quickly making their way Outside to begin a new life. Clarke, of course, spent decades as a West Coast logging photographer, but the Klondike had made its mark on Clarence. He gave up photography and mined throughout the territory--living in Dawson, Mayo and out along various creeks--for many years.

When there was no doubt that the population of the community was dwindling and Grand Forks would never be the rollicking town of a few years past, the North West Mounted Police gradually disbanded its regiment there. By 1909 only one Mountie of the Bonanza Detachment remained.

After following the Tanana mining boom to Fairbanks, Belinda Mulrooney Carbonneau and her husband left for the Outside in 1910 where they built a huge home

Clarke and his friend Asa Hayden pose for the camera before Clarke's departure from the Klondike in 1906.

known as "the Castle" in Yakima, Washington. She and the Count took winter trips to Europe and it was here that the couple invested and lost their entire fortune in a steamship company. Belinda died in 1967 at the age of 95, rich only in memories.

One by one the men and women of the Klondike had moved on, Jim Kingsley to Parksville, British Columbia and Ethel Russell to Fairbanks, Alaska, and later to Washington

This Klondike home on Highet Creek, circa 1910-15, was located in one of the many areas where Clarence and his family mined after leaving Grand Forks. Clarence finally moved back Outside in 1919, where he worked in a veterans' home near Seattle until 1949.

State. Some returned to their old lives as if they had never left. But if the experiences of the better known Klondike personalities are any proof, many lived these later years with a new kind of vigor, sometimes approaching recklessness--a bold confidence that came to those who had braved harsh winters, faced death and defied it, and built order in the midst of one of the wildest lands imaginable.

Even though profits could never amount to the fortunes that were made at the height of the gold rush, the dredging continued for nearly half a century. In 1921 an article from a Canadian newspaper mentioned that dredges had recently chewed their way through land where the downtown streets of Grand Forks once flourished.

In a 1956 issue of the *Snoqualmie Valley Record*, Clarke Kinsey's obituary briefly noted that he and his brother Clarence (who also died in 1956) had "operated a photography studio in Grand Forks, Yukon Territory, and also prospected for gold."

And for many who had spent the most difficult and exciting years of their life in the Klondike, such back-page newspaper items were the only tangible results to show for the experience. Yet for every fortune that wasn't made, another kind of reward was gained. The Klondike had turned ordinary people into heroes for a brief time and their stories, their recollections and the surviving Kinsey glass plate negatives have provided the epitaph for this remarkable period in history.

A sturdy cabin overlooks Number 6 Eldorado near downtown Grand Forks. Like all of the sluiceways and cabins perched along the creeks, it was dredged away a few years later.

99

Clarke's first son Leonard plays
with his father's camera. He
was born in Seattle on a trip
Outside in 1900 and died in
1907 of diptheria.

Two-story homes were rarities in the Klondike for many years.
The uncaptioned photograph above was probably taken by
Clarence after his brother left Grand Forks permanently for the
Outside. Once the photography business was dissolved, Clarence
took pictures for personal use, never bothering to caption them.

As shown by the calendar beneath the picture on the far wall, this
photograph of a Klondike dining room was taken in 1912.

Murray's Hotel was located at Number 33 Below on Lower Dominion, 37 miles from Dawson. One of the best roadhouses in the area, it had a pay phone, balcony and other rare conveniences. These establishments replaced the more elaborate hotels in downtown Grand Forks as the population dwindled.

Although this photograph, with its dark mine tunnel opening and bearded prospector in the foreground, seems to portray the early days of Klondike mining, it was actually taken in 1912. Clarence's brother-in-law, Bob Fisher, and other miners assemble around Olive Mineral Claim, named for Clarence's daughter Olive. Clarence often used the Kinsey and Kinsey label even after the partnership with Clarke ended; he and his wife Agnes took up photography under the Kinsey and Kinsey name as an avocation, rather than a business.

It seems that the Kinseys often cited records in their captions--records that are never quite verifiable. This load of wood was large, certainly, and wood was scarce from the beginning in the Klondike. By 1903, when this photo was taken, virtually all of the nearby hillsides had been logged out. And during the next few years, what little scrub trees or shrubs did exist vanished. The dredges took out everything in their path.

714

This dredge, assembled on site near downtown Grand Forks, was one of the earliest machines in operation. Note that much of the town remains intact. The largest of the dredges measured 68 by 136 feet and dragged up to 68 two-ton buckets through the dirt and gravel. These $500,000 machines weighed $4\frac{1}{2}$ million pounds each.

In 1904 Grand Forks was already experiencing an economic decline, but appeared to be flourishing with hotels lining the downtown streets and steepled churches at each corner of the community.

Long after dredges worked their way up and down Eldorado
and Bonanza creeks and through much of downtown, only
a few buildings in Grand Forks are left standing. The two-story
building appears to be the original Grand Forks Hotel, once
owned by Belinda Mulrooney. The hotel is the second building to
the right of Frank Clark's Drugstore in the opposite photo.

111

Sources

The research for *A Klondike Scrapbook* began in the 1970s with much of it accomplished somewhat by osmosis during the research and writing of *Klondike Lost: A Decade of Photographs by Kinsey & Kinsey* between 1978 and 1980.

While much has been written about the Klondike and the gold rush during the 80 years since this event took place, virtually nothing had ever been compiled on Grand Forks. Unfortunately there are no files labeled "Grand Forks" from which to gather information. Instead the history of the town and its inhabitants has been recounted through the Kinsey glass plate negatives, newspaper accounts of the day, Yukon government records, and, as mentioned earlier, the stories of those people still living who spent their childhood in Grand Forks.

All of the letters and many of the various records which have been reproduced in this book were found in the government records collections at the Yukon Archives, Whitehorse, Y.T. The staff at the Archives was extremely cooperative in helping sort through reams of handwritten letters, miscellaneous government memorandums and correspondence, and rolls of microfilm.

The many newspaper articles and excerpts used in the book were collected from various issues of *The Klondike News, The Klondike Nugget* and the *Dawson Daily News*. These issues, ranging in publication date from 1898 to 1912, are the property of the Seattle Public Library and the University of Washington Library in Seattle--or were made available through these institutions. The Alaska State Library in Juneau and the Dawson City Museum and Historical Society also proved very helpful in the search for relevant material on the Klondike.

Two noted historians have provided a valuable resource over the years. Robert N. DeArmond from Juneau, Alaska, is literally a walking encyclopedia of northern history, and time and again proved an invaluable friend and advisor. And finally, Pierre Berton is head and shoulders above the rest of the world in writing about the Klondike, and his guidance and input were extremely helpful in my work.

--Norman Bolotin